Yaralardan Yangın Doğar

Abhijit Naskar is a celebrated Neuroscientist, Bestselling Author of 100+ books, and the World's Beloved Poet of 1000+ sonnets, who has been serving at the forefront of humankind's struggle against hate, intolerance, bigotry and fanaticism.

Yaralardan Yangın Doğar

Explorers of Night are Emperors of Dawn

ABHIJIT NASKAR

Yaralardan Yangın Doğar: Explorers of Night are Emperors
of Dawn

An Amazon Publishing Company, 1st Edition, 2023

Printed in the United States of America

ISBN: 9798870183398

Also by Abhijit Naskar

The Art of Neuroscience in Everything
Your Own Neuron: A Tour of Your Psychic Brain
The God Parasite: Revelation of Neuroscience
The Spirituality Engine
Love Sutra: The Neuroscientific Manual of Love
Homo: A Brief History of Consciousness
Neurosutra: The Abhijit Naskar Collection
Autobiography of God: Biopsy of A Cognitive Reality
Biopsy of Religions: Neuroanalysis towards Universal
Tolerance
Prescription: Treating India's Soul
What is Mind?
In Search of Divinity: Journey to The Kingdom of Conscience
Love, God & Neurons: Memoir of a scientist who found
himself by getting lost
The Islamophobic Civilization: Voyage of Acceptance
Neurons of Jesus: Mind of A Teacher, Spouse & Thinker
Neurons, Oxygen & Nanak
The Education Decree
Principia Humanitas
The Krishna Cancer
Rowdy Buddha: The First Sapiens
We Are All Black: A Treatise on Racism
The Bengal Tigress: A Treatise on Gender Equality
Either Civilized or Phobic: A Treatise on Homosexuality
Wise Mating: A Treatise on Monogamy
Illusion of Religion: A Treatise on Religious
Fundamentalism
The Film Testament
Human Making is Our Mission: A Treatise on Parenting
I Am The Thread: My Mission
7 Billion Gods: Humans Above All
Lord is My Sheep: Gospel of Human
Morality Absolute
A Push in Perception
Let The Poor Be Your God
Conscience over Nonsense
Saint of The Sapiens
Time to Save Medicine

Fabric of Humanity
Build Bridges not Walls: In the name of Americana
The Constitution of The United Peoples of Earth
Lives to Serve Before I Sleep
When Humans Unite: Making A World Without Borders
All For Acceptance
Monk Meets World
Mission Reality
Citizens of Peace: Beyond The Savagery of Sovereignty
Operation Justice: To Make A Society That Needs No Law
See No Gender
The Gospel of Technology
Every Generation Needs Caretakers: The Gospel of
Patriotism
Aşkanjali: The Sufi Sermon
Mad About Humans: World Maker's Almanac
Revolution Indomable
When Call The People: My World My Responsibility
No Foreigner Only Family
Hurricane Humans: Give me accountability, I'll give you
peace
Ain't Enough to Look Human
Servitude is Sanctitude
Time To End Democracy: The Meritocratic Manifesto
I Vicdansaadet Speaking: No Rest Till The World is Lifted
Boldly Comes Justice: Sentient not Silent
Good Scientist: When Science and Service Combine
Sleepless for Society
Neden Türk: The Gospel of Secularism
Martyr Meets World: To Solve The Hard Problem of
Inhumanity
The Shape of A Human: Our America Their America
When Veins Ignite: Either Integration or Degradation
Heart Force One: Need No Gun to Defend Society
Solo Standing on Guard: Life Before Law
Generation Corazon: Nationalism is Terrorism
Mucize Insan: When The World is Family
Hometown Human: To Live For Soil and Society
Girl Over God: The Novel
Gente Mente Adelante: Prejudice Conquered is World
Conquered
Earthquakin' Egalitarian: I Die Everyday So Your Children
Can Live
Giants in Jeans: 100 Sonnets of United Earth

Vatican Virus: The Forbidden Fiction (Abi Naskar
Adventures Book 2)
Karadeniz Chronicle: The Novel (Abi Naskar Adventures
Book 3)
Şehit Sevda Society: Even in Death I Shall Live
Handcrafted Humanity: 100 Sonnets For A Blunderful
World
Mücadele Muhabbet: Gospel of An Unarmed Soldier
Making Britain Civilized: How to Gain Readmission to The
Human Race
Dervish Advaitam: Gospel of Sacred Feminines and Holy
Fathers
Honor He Wrote: 100 Sonnets For Humans Not Vegetables
The Gentalist: There's No Social Work, Only Family Work
Either Reformist or Terrorist: If You Are Terror I Am Your
Grandfather
Woman Over World: The Novel (Abi Naskar Adventures
Book 4)
High Voltage Habib: Gospel of Undoctrination
Bulldozer on Duty
Find A Cause Outside Yourself: Sermon of Sustainability
Ingan Impossible: Handbook of Hatebusting
Amor Apocalypse: Canım Sana İhtiyacım
Amantes Assemble: 100 Sonnets of Servant Sultans
Mucize Misafir Merhaba: The Peace Testament
Divane Dynamite: Only truth in the cosmos is love
Sin Dios Sí Hay Divinidad: The Pastor Who Never Was
Corazon Calamidad: Obedient to None, Oppressive to None
Esperanza Impossible: 100 Sonnets of Ethics, Engineering &
Existence
Mukemmel Musalman: Kafir Biraz, Peygamber Biraz
Himalayan Sonneteer: 100 Sonnets of Unsubmission
Yarasistan: My Wounds, My Crown
The Centurion Sermon: Mental Por El Mundo
Her Insan Ailem: Everyone is Family, Everywhere is Home
Humankind, My Valentine: World's First Anthology of 1000
Sonnets
Naskar's Knights: The Humanitarian Omnibus
Aşk Mafia: Armor of The World
Vande Vasudhaivam: 100 Sonnets for Our Planetary Pueblo
Visvavictor: Kanima Akiyor Kainat
Sapionova: 200 Limericks for Students
Rowdy Scientist: Handbook of Humanitarian Science
Insan Himalayanoğlu: It's Time to Defect

Tum Dunya Tek Millet: Greatest Country on Earth is Earth
Either Right or Human: 300 Limericks of Inclusion

DEDICATION

To every peacemaking civilian of earth.

CONTENTS

Part 1

Derviş biraz, kardeş biraz,
Sizin için ben kurban biraz.
Yangın biraz, rüzgar biraz,
Verdim sana her sevincim biraz.

To some I am dervish,
To some I am dynamite.
To some I am scientist,
To some I am cyanide.

I am no intellectual,
To be livid with logic.
I am no fundamentalist,
To act rigidly prehistoric.

I am no philosopher of the books,
To be enslaved by cultish ism.
I am no law-abiding citizen,
To comply with corrupt legalism.

I am the Dervish,
I am the Scientist;
Elixir to injury,
Cyanide to prejudice!

17

Part 2

Night brings light,
Injury brings elixir.
Gale delivers gallantry,
Clouds deliver character.

Paramparça olana kadar,
padişah olamazsın.
Till you are shattered,
you can't emerge sultan.

Everybody loves a good happily everafter,
While I am drawn to heartbreak stories.
Everybody is interested in your triumph,
I want to hear about your tragedies.

Karanlığın kaşifi şafağın kralıdır,
Yağmurun yolcusu yaraların galibidir.
Felaketten korkan herkes cenneti ister,
Cehenneme ışık getirir, cennetin sultan bir.

Cennet nedir biliyor musun?
Senin yüzünden insanlar gülümser
nereye, oraya senin cennetindir.

Artık sadece onu bulmak istiyorum,
Ona bir soru sormak istiyorum -
Cevabı, bir evet duymak istiyorum.

Then I remember,
this being is betrothed to humanity -
To ask for joy is civilian affair,
Sacrifice facilitates my felicity.

This is to reveal the human condition,
So you know there is no perfect human.
Even the saintliest of the reformer
has their own fair share of confusion.

Still it bothers me to expose my secrets
in the common language of our home planet.
You gotta go the extra linguistic miles,
to fathom the humanness of Mount Everest.

(Naskareans will find a way,
Come hail or high water!
Naskareans are never swayed,
by language, religion or culture.)

Naskar has never sought for recognition, neither should Naskareans. Work my soldiers, work - work for the welfare of this world with the last ounce of valiance in your veins. Only then shall you stand bold and proud, with a smile on your face, as a testament to my life. I don't want to live in my words - I want to live through you - I want you to be the proof that there ever was a human called Naskar. I exist, when you exist - as the absolute epitome of humanness possible - when you don't, I don't.

I don't want your allegiance - to me or anybody else! Allegiance is too petty a term to define what I want of you - for I don't want your allegiance - I want your annihilation - your absolute apocalyptic annihilation - for the ascension of humanity! Can you do that? Then what are you waiting for! Burn my books, and go lift the world! Let me live in your blood, not in books.

Yak benim her kitabımı, ve git - insanlara yardım et! Kitaplarda değil, kanında tut beni.

23

Part 3

There is no theory of everything,
because everything is a theory.
There is no perception of reality,
everything is perception, nothing is reality.

What you perceive becomes your reality,
What you believe becomes your reality.
Brain weaves its own fabric of truth,
Why not weave some delectable unity!

Facts are a state of matter,
Truth is a state of mind.
When hate is the global fact,
Love alone brings truth and light.

Love bears all difficulty,
Love defies all convenience.
You gotta be extremely irrational,
To chase your dream without bent.

Rationality bends under pressure,
Thought bends under pressure,
Intelligence bends under pressure -
Only love is crazy enough to stand unbent,
even under pressure of cataclysmic proportion.

Conscience, morality, justice, inclusion,
all these are but love's manifestation.
Intelligence is not the keynote here,
Intelligence enhances the application part,

but it's not the driver of illumination.

Trancewriting
(The Sonnet, 1258)

I don't like writing from thought,
Writing from thought is dull and boring.
It's when the subconscious does the writing,
That the words manifest magically awakening.

It takes some time to get used to,
You gotta trust your brain with the magic.
Lose yourself in your one chosen path,
Out pours the pearls of profundity terrific!

Let your subconscious do the writing,
Use thought afterwards to mend inaccuracy.
When absorbed in an unbending vision,
Like a ghost writes your mind almighty.

Most of my magic is born in transcendence -
Nothing paranormal, just atypical neuroactivity!
There is no spirit outside the domain of neurons,
We're just unaware of the extent of our capacity.

Part 4

There is a tangible explanation behind everything - whether you find it or not, depends on how far you are willing to go - how much hardship you are willing to bear - how many sleepless nights you are willing to embrace over a question - rather than simply give in to the convenience of comforting superstitions.

But then again, there are experiences to which we don't want an explanation, and that's perfectly fine - for example love - the least explained, the sweeter. But if it is really explanation we seek, then taking fiction as explanation is not understanding - it's the desecration of understanding.

So, I repeat, if you don't care for understanding, that's fine. But never designate your lack of understanding as the sign of higher understanding. We don't need to be logical all the time - in fact, it's good to be dumb at times - but don't confuse the absence of logic as extraterrestrial logic.

There is more to life than logic, but nothing alive is supernatural. There is more to

humanity than facts and figures, but nothing human is paranormal.
All these are matters of intellect - so, now let's come down to the ground of humanity. How do you treat those with a firm belief in the supernatural?

To which I say - why does it matter?

When I said, nothing human is paranormal, it meant, everything human is normal - that is, natural - you don't need the supernatural to explain any aspect of the human condition.

Belief in the supernatural doesn't make a person any less human. It is bigotry we must struggle against, not illogicality. So, even if you bear no affinity to any kind of supernaturalism yourself, that doesn't mean you oughta look down on those who do - and if you do look down on others for their apparently supernatural beliefs, then it is you who is the lesser human.

Call out supernaturalism that does harm, not supernaturalism in general. This is my law to my soldiers. Remember, it's more important to be kind than right. Your humanity is expressed through your behavior, not through your intellect.

That's why, I say, never glorify intellect, beyond the point of necessity. Logic is supposed to enhance life, not squeeze the sweetness out of life. That's why, great scientists are drawn to poetry and music, whereas mediocre, amateur and downright inferior scientists often diss the entire domain of arts.

Science on its own is earth-shaking, but science oxidized by poetry is dimension-bending. Philosophy on its own is eye-opening, but philosophy electrified by poetry is heartlifting.

So, let's continue with our poetic insanity, shall we! Because, it's only by being insane, we realize sanity.

33

Part 5

In those early days,
I gave you a motto -
My world, my responsibility.
I say to you further today,
Burn my books to cinders,
and go light up humanity.

Bu zor zamanda dünyanın
yeni peygamber sensin.
Hadi kalk be kardeşim, ve söz ver,
"Dünya benim, sorumluluk benim."

Mükemmel dünya diye hiç bir şey yok.
Dünya mükemmel doğmaz,
Dünyayı mükemmel yapmalısınız.
Mükemmel millet diye hiç bir şey yok.
Millet mükemmel doğmaz,
milletinizi mükemmel yapmalısınız.

English is my work language,
Turkish is my love language,
Spanish is my play language,
Telugu is my leisure language.

This would probably be different for you - perhaps for you, it all happens in one language - English, and that's perfectly fine. Different people are inspired in different ways - it's alright - as long as all our inspirations converge into one result - a better world for all - where there is no interracial dialogue, there is no intercultural communication, there is no interreligious relations - because - there is but one race, humanity - there is but one culture, humanity - there is but one religion, humanity.

My roots are grounded in humanity,
not in one culture or nation.
Cosmos courses through my corpuscles,
My life is a call to expansion.

Kral Fakir
(Servant King Sonnet, 1259)

İnsanı seven herkes resul,
Yardım eden herkes kraldır.
Bencil servet hayvanlara mübarek,
İnsan ben, kimliğim kral fakir.

Every human who loves a human is apostle,
Every human who helps a human is king.
Animals may feast on selfish luxury,
As for me, I am a servant king.

King is the servant,
Servant is king.
Being is the harvest,
Harvest is the being.

Life lived for self is goods,
Life lived for others is gift.
Time spent on self is product,
Time spent on others is present.

You can spend thousands on the shallow,
Still it won't be enough to fill their eyes.
Spend a single wise cent on someone in need,
It'll fill their heart with new vigor of life.

Part 6

Tiniest effort to lift the fallen,
Sets forth a chain reaction of uplift,
While all efforts to please the privileged,
Ultimately ends up meaning nothing.

As I said, and I repeat:
You can spend thousands of dollars on the shallow,
Still it won't be enough to light up their eyes.
But spend a single wise cent on someone in need,
It'll fill their heart with new vigor of life.

There is too much real suffering in the world,
Don't waste your energy on make believe misery.
Be aware, be brave, prioritize your attention;
Generosity must be practiced responsibly.

Careless generosity is generosity wasted,
Be a mindful monsoon drenching lives in drought.
I say, be aware, not cynical or skeptical,
Too much caution as well cripples thought.

What's needed is awareness not caution,
Caution causes anxiety, awareness ascension.
Keep caution lowest, and awareness fullest,
Awareness guides behavior towards illumination.

Mucize Mülteci
(Divine Refugee Sonnet, 1260)

Call me misafir, call me göçmen,
This heart of mine is always migrant.
Şan ve şöhrete ben muhtaç değilim,
Benim derdim dünya, dünya dermanım.

Call me gypsy, or call me refugee,
This heart of mine is always migrant.
I've got no use for silicon or gold,
World is my bane, world, my ointment.

In Sanskrit I am Abhijit,
In English I am Victor.
In Arabic I am Ghalib,
In History I am Reformer.

Call me whatever you like,
Befitting your culture.
I have no reservations,
Above my human nature.

So many tongues, as many names -
Some call agua, some call pani.
Conquer the tongue, spirit is the same -
Some dub it divine, I live as humanity.

43

Part 7

No matter my rational outlook of the universe as a scientist, I have great admiration for pastors who actively encourage their parishioners to look outside the christian tradition and garner a whole perspective of life. I feel a hearty closeness to these people of faith, which I cannot put in words. And believe you me, the number of such progressive faithworkers is increasing by leaps and bounds, which only reinforces my dream of a unified planet.

You see, rationality doesn't make you kind, but when you are kind you often end up behaving rational in the benefit of others, even if it goes against your doctrinal conditioning. This has nothing to do with intelligence, and everything to do with conscience - your living, breathing, original conscience.

Conscience is a compass born of kindness - where there is kindness, there is conscience - where there is no kindness, there is no conscience, no matter how intelligent you are. Intelligence makes you capable, kindness makes you human. Every computer is capable, no computer is human.

And in fact, it is this kindness that eliminates all vengeful elements from society. Kindness doesn't let you be vengeful, kindness doesn't let you be bitter - kindness guides you away from any path that might lead to bitterness.

Let me put this into perspective.

I don't approve of vengeful bitterness. If a person or nation does me wrong, I silently disappear from their life, rather than bearing a grudge to do wrong in return. Besides, I don't got time for bearing grudge and bitterness. Bitterness is too much of a burden, which I can do without - I got plenty real burdens of the world on my shoulders.

Several years back, after dumping me for an easier white, normal, native balkan alternative, someone said to me, "you won't do anything bad to me in revenge right!" I was devastated at the time - could barely write a word - and yet with a smile I responded - "even after spending over four years together, you still don't know me - what a shame!"

You see, back then I was still a struggling nobody - and it's easier for a white woman to be with a white nobody than a colored nobody - particularly in places where primitive stereotypes run deep, such as Eastern Europe.

Anyway, this wasn't the first time I was crushed. This time it was a person, before that, it was an entire nation. Many years back I had to break off all emotional dependency on a nation, because I did not want its mistreatment of me to turn me bitter or drive me in the path of vengeance.

You see, our vulnerability is our most priceless treasure. Be very careful with whom you share your vulnerability. Everyone deserves your kindness, not everyone deserves your vulnerability. Remember, it's not emotional maturity that facilitates bonding, it's emotional vulnerability.

Ask any random person, what do they look for in a partner – and most of them will say, emotional maturity. This is textbook shallowness. If we can't embrace each other's emotional vulnerability, we're better off with a hot water bottle. Vulnerability is the gateway to intimacy, not the so-called emotional maturity.

Part 8

Intimacy doesn't mean sharing nudity,
Intimacy means sharing vulnerability.
Any ape can be attracted to a naked body,
Takes a human to care for a naked psyche.

To wear simple, reveals a lot.
To live simple, feels a lot.
To own less, heals a lot.
To speak less, speaks a lot.

To say not, says a lot -
Mindful silence adds purpose to words.
To bend not, builds a lot -
Civilization corrupts through corrupt civilians.

I am not a rockstar,
I am a reformer.
Rockstars get compromised,
Uncompromise is my character.

There's too much hanging on my shoulders,
Upon individual integrity unfolds humanity.
Public scrutiny means nothing here,
What matters to me is my integrity.

I decide what's right, what's wrong,
With conviction, till death I stand strong.
Better die early with character intact,
Than keep lingering with virtues gone wrong.

Error is a natural part of life,
Correction is a civilized part of life.
In the world of nature everything is natural,
Everything natural isn't necessarily civilized.

Let me give you a simple example.

War is a natural part of the organic world,
It doesn't mean war can be accepted as civilized.
If we still cannot put down our weapons of war,
We're nothing more than warring animal tribes.

I have a clinical aversion to weapons,
Life is the antithesis of armament.
If disarmament seems impractical to you,
Don't you dare call yourself sapiens!

Human is the antithesis of vengeance,
Humanity is the antithesis of armament.
It has nothing to do with being nonviolent,
and everything to do with behaving human.

Your wound is my wound,
Your heartbreak is my heartbreak.
Iceage apes pleasure pouring salt,
To human wounds I am bandaid.

Only human is the bandaid,
Those carrying salt are animal.
Büyük bayramlar bile günah oldu,
Till a single person is in pain and trouble.

Du gamla, du fria -
När molnen skuggar,
Uppstå som levande Lucia!

55

Part 9

Broken bone heals back stronger,
Broken heart heals back braver.
Broken mind heals back wiser,
Broken life heals back brighter.

Brutet ben läker tillbaka starkare,
Brutet hjärta läker tillbaka modigare.
Brutet sinne läker tillbaka klokare,
Trasigt liv läker tillbaka ljusare.

Scars are not guilt marks,
Scars are mark of gallantry.
Scars are proof of resilience,
Scars are testament to bravery.

Scars are proof that you soldiered on,
Scars are proof that you never gave in.
Products are manufactured without scars,
People are shaped by scars and suffering.

Suffering is not a failure of life,
Suffering is a sign of life.
The living shall suffer one way or another,
So choose the reason, conscious and wise.

Hardship is a part of life,
Unless you have embraced your
existence of privileged slime.
Privileged or not doesn't matter,
Inheritance has no bearing on lifeline.

I have no work with those
obsessing over inheritance,
I work on humans not slime.
Consider yourself an orphan
when it comes to inheritance,
only then you might achieve
something worthwhile.

Consider yourself an orphan,
when it comes to identity,
only then can you grow the backbone,
to unleash your original humanity.

You don't know life
till you've known struggle.
Struggle to build your identity,
rather than crawling dead as
carbon copy ancestral.

Heritage is for the dead,
Inheritance is for vermin.
If you are alive and human,
Discard all this in the bin.

Heritage is obstruction to your humanity,
Inheritance is impediment to integrity.
If you wanna unfold a genuine character,
You gotta be an explorer of infinity.

Part 10

Rigidity fuels contraction,
Contraction fuels discrimination.
Rigidity facilitates prejudice,
Prejudice facilitates fragmentation.

Greed fuels inflation,
Inflation further sustains greed.
Greed powers disparities,
Disparities further sustain greed.

Unless we treat greed and shallowness first,
No policy can bring economic sustainability.
Increasing wages with increasing prices,
Do not pave the way for a sustainable society.

Let me elaborate with a thought experiment.

If suddenly one day, one after another new viral outbreaks start to appear, the right course of action is not to develop more and more new vaccines. We gotta develop new vaccines as a temporary fix to the problem, sure, but it's not the long-term solution. The long-term solution is to diagnose the root cause of the sudden outbreaks and eradicate that cause from our lifestyle. For example, if a newly acquired wild meat source is introducing previously unknown viruses to the human anatomy, then first and foremost, we gotta remove that food source from our diet. Likewise, only by treating greed and shallowness can we initiate real economic justice in society. We gotta treat the disease, not just the symptoms.

63

Part 11

Only by treating greed
can we bring lasting economic justice.
Only by treating indifference
can we bring lasting social justice.

Only by treating prejudice
can we eliminate bigotry.
Only by treating distance
can we eliminate discrimination.

Color doesn't define character, conduct does,
Wealth makes no individual, integrity does.
Clothes don't bring confidence, backbone does,
Belief doesn't determine worth, behavior does.

Obsessing over clothes is fashion,
Developing character is conscience.
To afford food is employment,
To afford principles is success.

Those who look the least successful,
are usually the most successful.
Successful people got no one to impress,
Only the mediocre behave all fanciful.

Look for the simplest person in the room,
they are usually the wisest in the room.
Suck up to the coolest person in the room,
they are usually the idiot in the room.

Look for the kindest people in the world,
they are usually the most capable sapiens.
Look for the aggressive people on earth,
they are the most uncivilized and incompetent.

Those who think aggression is a practical trait,
Deserve but absolute non-acknowledgment.
Those who think a nation is as strong as its military,
Belong in a mental hospital, not in government.

Part 12

Military is Legal Terrorism
(Ceasefire Sonnet, 1261)

Any planet that confuses guns
with gallantry is a planet of apes.
Prioritizing military over education,
we only build a world full of terrorists.

Military is just legal terrorism,
To fathom this you gotta be human.
What do monkeys know of peace and love,
When guns are their emblem of patriotism!

We don't need civilian disarmament,
We need absolute universal disarmament.
Only a worldwide ban on firearms production,
Can facilitate a paradigm of peaceful coexistence.

Let's see which nation has the heart and backbone,
To legislate absolute ban on firearms manufacture!
Let's see who are the first civilized people,
Let's see which nation is the first peacemaker!

What's the point of one ceasefire,
Let's pull the plug on all war.
Let's disband all military, and siphon
those funds to housing, education and healthcare.

El Ejército es Terrorismo Legal
(Soneto de Alto el Fuego)

Cualquier planeta que confunda armas
con valentía es un planeta de simios.
Al priorizar el ejército sobre la educación,
solo construimos un mundo de terrorismo.

El ejército es sólo terrorismo legal,
Para comprender esto hay que ser humano.
¡Qué saben los monos de la paz y el amor,
Cuando las armas son emblema del patriotismo!

No necesitamos el desarme civil,
Necesitamos un desarme universal absoluto.
Sólo una prohibición mundial de la producción de armas,
Puede facilitar un paradigma de convivencia pacífica.

¡Veamos qué nación tiene el corazón y conciencia,
Para legislar prohibición absoluta de las armas!
¡Veamos quiénes son la primera gente civilizada,
Veamos qué nación es la primera pacificadora!

¿Para qué sirve un alto el fuego?
¡Acabemos con toda guerra!
Disolvamos todos los militares,
y desviamos ese dinero a vivienda,
educación y atención médica.

You cannot force peace,
Peace comes from within.
So long as there is
even a speck of cynicism,
no peace is ever coming.

I don't write to force you listen,
I write for those who want to listen.
I don't write to force the way of love,
I write for those already in lovelane.

I don't mind if you burn my books,
In fact, I'd prefer you to burn my books.
When each individual becomes a moral fountain,
There'll be no need for more philosophy cooks.

Tell me you shall stand up to injustice 'n prejudice,
and embrace scientific evidence without resistance,
and I shall retire tomorrow - in peaceful contentment.

73

Part 13

The day you learn to question yourself,
No more you'll need to outsource philosophy.
The day you become your own constitution,
No more you'll need no second-hand society.

Civilized parameters come from self-discovery,
Life can't be contained in dead conformity.
Just Poetry or Poetic Justice,
I don't know what I write - all I know is,
No description does justice to the sun's majesty.

Description stands as hindrance to the act,
Assumption stands as hindrance to illumination.
Profiling stands as hindrance to understanding,
Judgmentality keeps the creature from being human.

Let me give you an example.

To assume every woman is out to dig for gold,
is not masculinity, it's simian masculinity.
Likewise, to assume every man is a sexist pig,
is not feminism, it's canine femininity.

Never be obsessed with any ism to such an extent,
that you lose touch with decency and common sense.
Place your attention on rights and equality,
not on ideological parameters of imaginary sense.

Slaves of ideology can never be advocates
of humanity, let alone practitioner.
Unless you are absolutely free from ism,
you only trade in one blindness for another.

Fight for rights and equality, yes,
That's the human thing to do,
But never under the banner of ism,
For isms are the root of all doo-doo.

Thus, even activism can become
an impediment to true human rights struggle.
When ideology clouds your conscience,
You won't even know when you behave animal.

Vicdansız zeka sadece zehirdir,
İnsansız hayat sadece haramdir.
Inteligencia sin conciencia es demencia,
Aplica tu cerebro con la humanidad.

Cleverness without conscience is poison,
Cleverness without conscience is calamity.
Life without people is damnation,
Human without humanity is a divine tragedy.

Correct your ways the moment they tend to turn cold - because no matter how advanced you think you are in intellectual intervention, if you lose your everyday ordinary touch with the soil and society, all your intellect, all your education, all your high and mighty learnedness are worth nothing.

I am not saying that you can't make mistakes - of course you can - in fact, you will - a lot of them. But remember this - worth of a mistake lies in the lesson. Mistakes are nothing to be ashamed of, they are just part of growth - that's all.

Mistakes you make during your struggles, are not the shame of your life, they are the cornerstones of clarity and conviction. Never try to hide your imperfect past, trying to adapt to perfectionist fantasy. Machines are produced in the assembly line, without past, without flaws, not life.

79

Part 14

Live by body,
Die by body.
Live by mind,
Never die.

Death comes but once,
Life comes every day.
Now tell me what's braver,
Spirit of life or fear of death!

There is no afterlife,
because there is no after,
there is only life now.
To live life conquering fear,
is the ultimate divine vow.

Be humble and live simple,
That's the route to wholeness -
Whole and humble ends all race.

Life is not a race,
Life is a delectable mess.
Only the brave and mighty,
one with conscientious dignity,
can carve meaning out of the mess.

There is meaning in every mess,
There is mess behind every meaning.
Meaning and mess are states of mind;
Reduce the clutter, meaning starts pouring.

Bravely march into mess,
and emerge with meaning!
Cowardice may suit the apes,
on humans it's most unbecoming.

Conquest of fear is the beginning of life,
There is no life while fear is dominant.
Conquer your fear with a backbone of steel,
All inhumanities are but fear's descendant.

Let me put this into perspective
with one such stereotypical fear,
which has been propagated worldwide,
primarily by American cinema and media.

Before you assume like a moron,
all muslims are terrorists,
remember, Naskar is a muslim poet.
Naskar is sufi, Naskar is advaitin -
Naskar is all, in a humanitarian scientist.

Part 15

Ever since the emergence of the concept of state, propaganda has kept humans from becoming human. And what is the greatest carrier of propaganda? Cinema - cinema is the most effective carrier of propaganda in history. That's how Hollywood has been poisoning the world against the Middle East and China, just like Bollywood has been poisoning its citizens against Pakistan.

Sure, both Hollywood and Bollywood have created good cinema as well, but the evil they've propagated far outweighs the good - particularly Hollywood. Peddle the same narrative of hate and fear over and over to the masses, and eventually the ape brains of the masses adopt that narrative as the baseline of all thinking. It's not magic, just animal psychology 101. It doesn't help to have a nation full of freethinkers, because freethinkers cannot be scared easily - and if you cannot sell fear to the citizens, you'll soon run out of business, whether you are in the business of news, entertainment or government.

Neither propaganda nor tradition
can control a sentient person,
who has renounced all rigidity,
and rejected social castration.

When fear reigns sanity supreme,
prejudice deemed consciousness,
all breath becomes futile air,
all heart is rendered pulseless.

When air becomes breath,
and cells become sentient,
Words become poetry,
and facts become science.

Mind is the tether between facts and science,
Mind is the line of life between words and poetry.
People are the tether between mind and meaning,
Soil is the tether between human and humility.

87

Part 16

Closer to soil,
more the humility -
Further you drift apart,
more you're enamored with cruelty.

Thus the entire world turns into a madhouse,
Where ceasefire and disarmament are taboo.
When government institutions hold more lunatics
than mental institutions, know that,
no democracy will ever make peace come true.

When government institutions hold more lunatics than mental institutions, know that, there's something clinically wrong with this world. And the irony is, most political lunatics may not be fundamentally inhuman like Donald Duck, but indifference and unaccountability of the humans do more damage than the active animality of the inhumans.

However, the real grey area here is this. The obvious rebel in you would automatically jump to the same old baseless assumption that I'm talking about overthrowing the government. So let me put it bluntly. Overthrowing the government solves nothing

- overthrow one government, another bunch of incompetent fools will take its place – if not, there will be complete and utter chaos. Hence, the goal is not to overthrow the government, but to render government useless. And the only way we can render government useless, is to renounce the delegation and reclaim the duties.

And if you are still wondering, where does it all begin?

Well, there's a variety of ways to reclaim your duties to the world. I cannot spoonfeed you the methods as well - instead, I'll point out one real-life example.

I own just two 5 dollar tshirts - one is my regular wear, another my backup for washdays. And for my travels I own two 10 dollar shirts and two 20 dollar jeans, which are also used for my book covers. I don't need more, I don't buy more. This is not minimalism, it's called self-regulation - the lack of which has led to the shallow, judgmental, privilege-craving prick of a society we live in today. It's not about saving money, it's about humanizing money, by using it wisely, not just for individual benefit, but collective benefit.

Buy the things you need the most, save a little for rainy days, and use the rest to lift up the fallen. Any citizen who masters this simple humanitarian habit, is no longer obligated to pay taxes to the government. And when enough citizens of the world make it the mantra of their life, not just to lift themselves, but each other, the governments of the world are automatically rendered obsolete.

Government is funded by the people - then the governments use those funds to manufacture war, in order to further sustain the democratic cashflow that keeps them in business. Therefore, when people pull their funds and redirect them themselves, towards actual, tangible, humanitarian initiatives, there isn't going to be a government. It's only the humanitarian indifference of the citizens that keeps governments alive, that in turn keep borders and wars alive. Once the citizens are actually, genuinely, nontheoretically accountable of the welfare of society, beyond the prehistoric paradigm peddled by the state, all Capitol, Kremlin and White Hall will crumble to dust.

Part 17

Guns Are Viagra
(Sonnet 1262)

Indifference does more damage than inhumanity,
For animals can't be expected to be human.
Humans are human when they are accountable,
Passive spectators are worse than inhuman.

Silence of the peacelovers is more damaging
than violence of the warmongers.
Till the very thought of guns makes you sick,
you are only playing make believe peacekeepers.

Guns are just viagra for the impotent,
Bullets are but crutches for centipedes.
When there's no substance in mind and spine,
Monkeys tend to cower behind semiautomatics.

More backward a country,
more its fascination with guns and bombs.
That's why you cannot imagine a hero,
without a gun in their hands.

Real heroes don't carry guns,
Real heroes don't wear capes.
Wearing a smile, carrying a spine,
Real heroes work to rescue peace,
from the clutches of states.

97

Part 18

Freedom is never given,
You gotta snatch it from the oppressor.
With peace, humankind is the oppressed,
and all states are oppressor.

You gotta rescue peace from the states,
For no state will ever organize peace.
No matter their lies of peace and harmony,
Inside, all states are merchants of malice.

All states are born of nationalism,
How can something so primitive
achieve anything civilized!
Ceasefire is never given,
You gotta seize it from the termites!

Rescue love from the clutches of hate,
Rescue peace from the clutches of state.
Rescue inclusion from the clutches of habit,
Rescue humanity from the clutches of apes.

Over the years I have walked and explored various uncharted territories of integration, but for some inexplicable reason (or perhaps not so inexplicable at that, to those who are well aware with the origin of Naskar), I find myself drawn back to my psychological homebase - to my original intervention - the original purpose for which Naskar was born - the purpose of religious assimilation.

That is why, atheism has never been the focus in any of my work. If your own exploration of nature and the universe makes you outgrow the influence of ancestral myths, that's great - if not, it doesn't matter to me one bit. So long as you are a decent human being, your psychological necessity of a personal deity or the lack of it, is irrelevant outside your personal life.

If you stop believing in God, that won't magically make you a better person than you already are - in the same way - if you start believing in God, it won't magically make you a better person than you already are. Neither faith nor intellect makes a person good - if a person is good, they know how to use their faith or intellect for good.

So, I repeat, what's needed, is not the end of religion, but the end of religious intolerance.

Part 19

Before you are an intellectual, be a human,
Before you are a believer, be a human.
Before you are a rationalist, be a human,
Before you're a person of faith, be a human.

A rigid adherence to a religious identity only diminishes a person's human identity. In the same way, too much attachment to the intellectual identity, often ruins the sweetness of human identity, by disconnecting the mind from everyday ordinary human life. Let's take the idealistic notion of career woman, for example.

If a woman chooses to gives up their career to start a family, that's their choice. They are not taking a pause from life, they are simply choosing a life different from the new norm, that is, the life of a career woman. If, as a woman, you can manage both career and family, that's fantastic! But don't go about imposing your idealistic beliefs on women who choose to trade in career for family. If you do, you are no different from those traditionists of toxic masculinity. Remember, the solution to toxic masculinity is not toxic femininity - where either you are a career woman or you have no worth in society.

Until recently, career women were frowned upon, and those who stayed at home were respected - now the situation has gotten reversed - not better mark you, just reversed. Now career women are respected, and those who give up their career, or step down to a less demanding position, in order to raise a family, are object of ridicule. This is not progress, it's recurring regress. Substituting one authoritarian cruelty with another is not progress, it's recurring regress - which is also the case when you ban hijab in the name of freedom.

In a family, who is the principle provider and who is the principle carer - or whether both partners share the responsibilities equally, is the decision of the couple themselves, and nobody else. Neither conservatism nor idealism has a say in it. Control is the enemy here, not tradition.

All this time tradition has been the primary vessel for control, but now, intellectual idealism is taking over that role. This won't do. We must learn to be human, rather than puppets of tradition or robots of intellect.

Remember, cruelty of concrete is just as heartbreaking as cruelty of the jungle. It's not enough to change things, we must change things for the better, otherwise, why change at all! If all we do is replace old cruelty with new ones, then what's the point of such change!

The world of justice is extremely grey. Each act of justice is liable to create a whole new strain of injustice, unless you are careful. And the irony is - you won't even be aware of the new injustice that you end up causing yourself, in the name of ending old injustice.

In short, beware my friend! In an attempt to end conservative darkness, you better not become the merchant of newage darkness. Remember, all darknesses in history were caused by people who thought they were bringing light.

Part 20

There is nothing more ominous
than counterfeit light,
There is nothing more unjust
than counterfeit justice.

There is nothing more ignorant
than counterfeit knowledge,
There is nothing more unfree,
than counterfeit liberty.

There is no greater failure
than a success that ruins your humanity,
There is no greater tragedy
than a triumph erected upon cruelty.

Now we gotta ask a quintessential question. What is triumph? Or simpler still - what is success?

If we submit to the rotten guidelines of a rotten society, then success is nothing but a measure of monetary value. And nothing could be farther from the truth. Money is not the measure of success. Then what is, one wonders!

To be able to answer this, you gotta ask yourself, what is a good life? And more importantly, what are the fundamental requirements of a good life? Once you get a grip over the fundamental requirements of a good life, only then shall you understand the true meaning of success.

For example, if you are struggling to make ends meet, you do not have the luxury to decline any job, even if it clashes with your ideals. What does this mean? It means that, first you gotta surpass the struggle of making ends meet - with the last drop of your sweat.

Struggle hard, not to earn a lot of money, but to earn a position - a distinct identity, which is no longer influenced by pettifoggery.
Work hard, my friend, so you could afford some dignity! Work hard, not to be rich, but to be self-sufficient, so that you could refuse a well-paid job on moral grounds.

Success doesn't mean the accumulation of wealth - being rich and being successful are not the same thing. Success is a state of mind, riches are a state of money. If you can afford to put principles before profit, you are plenty successful alright - even if you are not super rich.

To afford food is employment, to afford principles is success. To earn money is employment, to earn morality is success. But be aware, neither employment not success is inferior or superior to the other. If anything, they supplement each other - they compliment each other - they are intertwined with each other.

A lot of idealistic intellectuals shout from their ivory tower of heartless intellectualism - "principles come first". I say to you - food come first, principles second - particularly if you have a family to support. Bookish intellectuals utter a lot of idealistic nonsense, which has no relation to everyday ordinary human life. Don't take them seriously - you do what you gotta do.

Let me put it to you bluntly. First responsibility, then morality. Chasing after morality or dreams without first tending to the practical necessities of life, is not courage, it's baseless stupidity. People who are not born into privilege do not have such luxury.

Dreams are important, but if the pursuit of dreams turns you into a heartless monster - unaware of responsibilities, unaware of the conditions of people around you, particularly your loved ones, then such dreams are not worth a single penny.

You cannot be a good dreamer, unless you are a good provider – and if you cannot provide even the basic amenities, then do not start a family till you can. Let's take entrepreneurship for example. You cannot be an entrepreneur, unless you are a good provider. As a 9 to 5 person, your family is your responsibility, as an entrepreneur the families of your employees are your responsibility, as well as the welfare of your customers or clients.

Responsibility is the key to better society, not revenue. Remember that. Whether you do a 9 to 5 job or own a business, you can never be a successful professional, unless you embrace and carry your responsibilities with some dignity.

Your professional stature does not determine whether you are successful. You can be a big shot entrepreneur, worth billions of dollars, and still be a failure as a person - at the same time, you can do an ordinary 9 to 5 job with a modest salary, and be the very pinnacle of success in your society.

Today who abandons their family for their entrepreneurial dream, tomorrow will abandon their employees when that dream goes bankrupt. Because these people only care about one thing - themselves. And success and selfishness are antithesis of each other. That's why, only the dutybound can lead a successful life.

Integrity is needed, dutyboundedness is needed, responsibleness is needed - these are

the ingredients that make character. Where there is character, there is success - no character, no success.
Practicality and principles must go hand in hand. One cannot be compromised for the other. A good life is rooted in moderation. Now please don't intellectualize this with all sorts of fancy terms like "minimalism". What I am talking about is rather simple.

Be aware of your necessities. Learn to distinguish between necessity and luxury. Most of the disparities and depressions in the world are caused in the pursuit of luxury. It takes very little to lead a good life, but a life of luxury is essentially a breeding ground of anxiety, shallowness, misdemeanor, recklessness, and all sorts of mental and social ailments.

That is why, for success to be sustainable, it must be rooted in simplicity. Unless your success is rooted in simplicity, it is but a passing cloud. Be simple, be humble, be responsible - that's all you need to be successful, impactful, and above all, characterful.

Part 21

There is no greatness without accountability and discipline - or simpler still - there is no civilized life without accountability and discipline. You can chase the allure of freedom and liberty all you want, but if you don't know how to practice that liberty wisely, then that liberty will do more damage than lack of liberty.

If you don't want to rely on external parameters of morality and principles, you must be civilized enough to draw your own parameters - and practice your own sense of self-regulation when you tend to go astray. You must be your own guiding angel - which means, you gotta refuse yourself certain endeavors that fall outside your self-drawn moral parameters.

Civilized is not the one who has no moral parameters - civilized is the one who is sentient enough to write their own parameters, rather than rely on old run-down institutions and traditions. As I've made it clear many a times - I am not saying, everything old is wrong, but just because it's old and traditional, doesn't make it right. It's not about rejecting the old, it's about rejecting allegiance to the old, as well as recklessness of the new.

Be an explorer - but not a reckless explorer - be a responsible explorer - who is well aware of the implications of their exploration, and mends their footsteps towards a humane future - not an exciting future, but a humane future.

Be human first, then everything you do will bring the necessary advancement, both internally and externally. Persist, persist and persist - persist in the path of humanness - everything else is unimportant.

Even when your peers coerce you to walk down the roads of misdemeanor with them, you gotta stand strong on your conviction. Remember, once you give in, giving in becomes a habit - then in time, that individual habit becomes a social norm. Which means, to break the cycle, you gotta stand your ground, despite all the coercion and self-absorption that is rampant in society.

Part 22

Live like you are society, that is,
Be the walking specimen of society,
not the one you live in,
but the one you want to live in.

Live not like you own the world,
Live like you are the world.
Live not like you are a law-abiding citizen,
Live like your accountability is the law.

Jehovah, Krishna or Avengers,
Your belief counts for nothing.
Higher than myths, both old and new,
It's behavior that makes the being.

I am not a STEM advocate,
I am the STEM humanizer.
I am not a faith advocate,
I am the faith humanizer.

Behavior is my priority,
Reason and faith are mere accessory.
Reason and faith don't come with heart,
Your heart is the root of all melody.

Give Me A Keyboard,
I'll Give You Revolution
(The Sonnet, 1263)

I just want to write -
that's all I ever want -
to write, write and write!
The day the words stop coming,
will be my last corporeal night.

Either I shall die by an assassin's bullet,
or I shall die on my keyboard,
but I refuse to die of old-age and disease.
Death scares those who are scared of life,
I have already lived my life in service.

I live on keyboard, I'll die on keyboard,
Keyboard is my instrument of illumination.
Nothing short could satisfy my palate -
Give me a keyboard, I'll give you revolution.

With my keyboard I've defended the meek,
With my keyboard I've castrated the pricks.
With my keyboard I've brought down dictators,
With my keyboard I've schooled bigoted pigs.

With my keyboard I've raised Gods by hundreds,
With my keyboard I've delivered world-builders.
With my keyboard I've produced hatebusters,

With my keyboard I've raised bulldozers.

Death is but a myth - body dies, not bulldozer;
Body is merely a vessel for the mission.
If you want your ideas to live forever,
You gotta sacrifice your life for a vision.

I never lived as body, but only as a dream -
My life is testament to the dream of united earth.
I don't have a message, for I am the message -
Sacrifice is beacon, that illuminates the universe.

127

Part 23

Be a swan amidst swine,
Be water amidst wine.
When all be walking veggies,
Unleash your upright spine.

Spine is the load bearing pillar,
While heart is but the foundation -
Brain is the craftsman visionaire,
Wielding all three comes ascension.

All three are essential,
to facilitate civilized behavior.
Absence of any one of these,
could essentially lead to disaster.

Heart, brain and spine -
all combined, a being emerges whole.
Wholeness bears the seed of civilization,
all others are mere garbage plated with gold.

Often the greyness of the world compels a person to behave most uncivilized. And this is possible particularly when the person has an underdeveloped wholeness, due to various sociological reasons. Thus, the person ends up committing many heinous misdeeds - often by mistake.

Let me put this into perspective.

No innocent must die, no matter the cause. I don't approve of it when a teenage Indian freedom fighter from Bengal blew up a carriage with two innocent british women, mistaking it to be carrying a british judge - I don't approve of it when Guevara's rage against imperialism put many innocents to death, out of sheer suspicion - and I don't approve of it today. In your fight against the oppressor, if you end up inflicting harm on the innocent, then you are no better than the oppressor you fight against - no matter your intention or cause.

However, one thing we must acknowledge. It was a much greyer times back then, than it is today. Hence, we cannot judge the old world based on the standards of the new world, any more than we can judge the new world based on the standards of the old world. But the point is this - each generation's struggle for justice and equality leaves behind a less grey world for the next generation. Mark you, they'll still have to deal with a lot of greyness of their own, for there never will be a black and white world. Never! The greyness will always remain - all we can do is, acknowledge the greyness around, and endeavor to treat it, rather than, mollycoddling the greyness with a lot of make believe, in the name of tradition.

Traditions are like training wheels - it provides stability during your developing years, but you can't live on training wheels forever. Once you start to think and feel for yourself, you gotta get rid of the training wheels, otherwise, they become the greatest impediment to life.

But mark you, don't go taking this literally, and assume, everything about tradition is bad, hence must be fought against at all cost. That's not the case. What this means is that, you gotta break free from the hypnotism of tradition, so that you can recognize and embrace the good of tradition, while rejecting the bits that cause harm.

So I say again, it's all about wholeness. It's about developing wholeness, it's about practicing wholeness, it's about living as a whole human being - aware of everything, accountable of everything, and obedient to nothing. But don't confuse this with rebellion, for it has nothing to do with rebellion, and everything to do with accountability. Reform is an act of accountability, not rebellion.

133

Part 24

Often rebellion is confused with revolution, and that's how an intelligent lifeform brings down its own doom - all in the name of advancement. The most apt example of this, would be the over-glorification of Artificial Intelligence.

You see, Artificial Intelligence is nothing new - the day we harnessed electron, was the beginning of artificial intelligence. However, over time as the mechanism underneath got more complex and sophisticated, the resulting technology became exponentially more potent. As a matter of fact, with recent advancements in both analogue and digital engineering, technology has developed powers of apocalyptic proportions. And the problem is, though technology has developed powers of apocalyptic proportions, the human mind wielding those powers are the same old primitive brutes from the jungle, whose primary motivation in life is still greed.

Hence, it is only likely, that such limitless technological advancement will do more damage than good, in the long run. For example, the brutes have already started to use generative AI to produce fake content and disinformation, which no ordinary consumer can recognize to be fake.

Then there are the frauds who take credit for AI generated content. It is this simple - if you use AI to write poetry, you are not a poet - if you use AI to write music, you ain't no composer - if you use AI to tune your voice, you ain't no singer - just like, if you use stunt doubles to do your stunts, you don't deserve an ounce of respect as an actor – use stunt doubles to teach you those stunts instead, then do them yourself on camera.

Does this mean that, AI generated content is fundamentally a bad thing? Definitely not! For example, there is nothing wrong in setting up an entire new genre of well moderated AI generated content in every industry, if you like AI content so much - but when humans take credit for the AI creation, it's not creativity, it's plain, old, petty, run-of-the-mill fraud - no matter how you try to peddle it with fancy labels.

We stand at a crucial moment in human evolution - a moment that will have far reaching implications upon the very paradigm of truth and reality. The brain is biased by default to begin with - on top of that, if you flood it with more lies, then I'm afraid, within a hundred years human creativity will be scarcer than a western nation without racism.

That's why I say, my friend - develop your conscience. Because without conscience, you won't know what honor is - and when you don't know what honor is, you won't even know when you start drifting into the world of fraudulence yourself.

Without discipline you'll accomplish nothing,
Without conscience you are nothing.
Without vision all zeal is misleading,
Without awareness all existence is degrading.

To make noise is not life,
Life is to make music.
Shallow flesh makes plenty noise -
Muster substance, and lo pours music!

Create less, but create with substance -
Live every moment with substance.
It's not the length of breath that counts,
it's the depth of life's intent.

Cowards dream of long life,
Bravehearts just wanna die with dignity.
One day of a braveheart's existence
holds more life than a coward's century.

The world is evolutionarily programmed
to facilitate either cowardice or cruelty,
Yet you got all the potential in your cells
to be the brave mutation of magnanimity.

I choose peace, not because I don't know violence -
I choose peace, because I know too much violence.
Only when we acknowledge our violent streak,
can we embody collective liberty, wielding sapience.

Part 25

The Gaza Sonnet, 1264
(All Free or None Free)

Al-Shams to Alpha Centauri,
All occupied lands will be free.
Till there is smile on every face,
All happiness is blasphemy.

Happiness is not an imperial merch,
Freedom is no colonizer's heirloom.
Joy is no bigot's ancestral bequest,
Earth is not a zionist hand-me-down.

Divide and rule is the law of animals,
Unite and integrate is law of humanity.
One human life is worth more,
than all the gas reserves underneath.

Gaza is not a place, Gaza is a wake up call,
to the peace-crying humanity.
Awake, Arise, O Citizens of Earth -
Till all of us are free, none of us are free!

No state cares for a profitless state - people might, individuals might, but not states. People might care about other people, regardless of profitability, but no government ever aids another government out of sheer goodwill, unless there is some form of benefit, which is rarely obvious to the general public.

Governments don't exist to do what's right, governments exist to do whatever increases their chances to stay in power for another term - not this government or that government, but every government.

Therefore, never - I repeat, never, ever put neither faith nor absolute reliance on government, whether your own or another. As I have said over and over - all my hopes and dreams are predicated on everyday, ordinary civilians. From the civilians will come my soldiers - from the civilians will come my humanitarians - from the civilians will come my world builders and peacemakers.

Part 26

Sonnet 1265

There is no such thing as world leaders,
There is only world citizens.
There is no such thing as UN peacekeepers,
There is only peacemaking civilians.

From the civilians emerge humanitarians,
From the civilians emerge world builders.
From the civilians emerge heartlifters,
From the civilians emerge bridge builders.

Don't put your faith on law and policy -
Person is the law, person is the policy.
Order cannot be installed by external means,
All order is fake, if there's no accountability.

Individual accountability brings collective growth,
The collective is but a reflection of the individual.
Wielding the powers of heart, brain and backbone,
Civilian intervention is the ultimate intervention.

Citizenry is the problem,
Citizenry is the answer.
When citizenry decides on peace,
Albeit reluctant, world leaders wither.

I know no constitution but conscience,
I know no tradition but compassion.
Belonging is my Bible, kindness is my Quran -
The living need no handbook to right and wrong.

Recognition or no recognition,
Human never forgets to be human.
The entire Abhijit Naskar legacy
was created without any recognition.

Then why did I continue you ask,
Because I never wrote for admiration.
I write to provide shelter to all,
And electrify their veins into action.

Whining might suit the spineless,
Bravehearts are ever vigilant in duty.
Once you make people your life's cause,
Nothing can diminish your tenacity.

My Pronoun is People
(Inclusivity Sonnet, 1266)

My pronoun is people,
I'm divergent, yet invincible.
I am straight, I am queer;
I am civilian, I am seer.
Spirit of life, I - am universal!

Call me disabled or differently able,
Call me collective or individual.
Fleshly forms I've got plenty,
All run by same love and liberty -
Culture supreme is inclusion.

Each heart is a shelter for another,
Each life is sanctuary for another.
Blasting all traditions of divide
into cinders with knowledge-dynamite,
we shall emerge as each other's keeper.

You ask, what am I - I say, I am human,
Better yet, I'm human's idea of a human.
I am but the human absolute -
morally unbending 'n divinely cute -
ever evolving testament to expansion.

Expansion brings accountability,
Accountability facilitates expansion.
Inclusion is a byproduct of expansion,
Where there is expansion, there is union.

Inclusion is just a fancy term for love,
World of love is world inclusive.
And how do you build bridges of love?
You don't - you just raise no walls divisive.

세상은 사랑, 사랑은 세상;
너의 고통은 나의 고통.
지성은 도움, 사랑은 존재;
오늘의 희생이 내일의 문명.

(Sesang-eun salang, salang-eun sesang;
Neoui gotong-eun naui gotong.
Jiseong-eun doum, salang-eun jonjae;
Oneul-ui huisaeng-i naeil-ui munmyeong.)

نہیں۔ مذہب کوئی بڑا سے انسانیت
نہیں۔ وجود کوئی بڑا سے محبت

You don't cause inclusion, inclusion is already there -
You just bring down the barriers within.
You don't make peace, for peace is already there -
You just bulldoze the impediments to smithereens.

Part 27

Expansion, expansion, expansion - that's the motto. With expansion will come the right order - with expansion will come the right education - with expansion will come the right civilization. You won't have to force it - you won't have to legislate it - you won't have to police it. It'll all be normal, ordinary civilian habit, just like people go for a jog everyday, out of their own free, without needing the law to tell them, it's the right thing to do.

Law is becoming more and more punishment centric, rather than education centric. It's not law and order, it's law and disorder. Education is becoming more and more competition centric, rather than curiosity centric. It's not education, it's castration.

Machines are becoming more and more comfort centric, rather than solution centric. It's not artificial intelligence, it's artificial paralysis. It's not technological advancement, it's the technological equivalent of white privilege.

Life is becoming more and more luxury centric, rather than meaning and purpose centric. It's not life, it's breakdown in the making. Personality is becoming more and more body centric, rather than behavior centric. It's not personality, it's primitivity.

The body is just a costume, it's ideas that make the character. And I am not talking about all that reincarnation or life after death nonsense - no - I am talking about something much simpler and yet, which takes much more courage. I am talking about immersing yourself so deeply in ideas, that those ideas become your life. If you can do that, only then, long after your body has dissipated in nature, every time people contemplate those ideas, someone, somewhere will bring up your name. That's real immortality - that's real life - that's real existence - beyond body, beyond time, beyond space.

153

BIBLIOGRAPHY

Archer M., (2000), Being Human: The Problem of Agency. Cambridge University Press.

Adolphs R (2003) Cognitive neuroscience of human social behaviour. Nature Rev Neurosci 4: 165–178.

Adolphs R, Tranel D, Damasio AR (2003) Dissociable neural systems for recognizing emotions. Brain Cogn 52: 61–69.

Andresen, Jensine, and Robert Forman, eds. Cognitive Models and Spiritual Maps. Bowling Green, Ohio: Imprint Academic, 2000.

Bernstein R.J., (1971), Praxis and Action: Contemporary Philosophies of Human Activity. Philadelphia: University of Pennsylvania Press.

Bernstein R.J., (1976), The Restructuring Social and Political Thought.

Bogen, J.E.(1995a), 'On the neurophysiology of consciousness: Part I. An overview', Consciousness and Cognition, 4.

Bogen, J.E. (1995b), 'On the neurophysiology of consciousness: Part II. Constraining the semantic problem', Consciousness and Cognition, 4.

Bremner, J. D., R. Soufer, et al. (2001). "Gender differences in cognitive and neural correlates of remembrance of emotional words." Psychopharmacol Bull 35 (3).

Brothers, L. (2002). The social brain: A project for integrating primate behavior and neurophysiology in a new domain. In J. T. Cacioppo et al. (Eds.), Foundations in neuroscience. Cambridge, MA: MIT Press.

Buss, D. D. (2003). Evolutionary Psychology: The New Science of Mind, 2nd ed. New York: Allyn & Bacon.

Buss, D. M. (1989). "Conflict between the sexes: Strategic interference and the evocation of anger and upset." J Pers Soc Psychol 56 (5).

Buss, D. M. (1995). "Psychological sex differences. Origins through sexual selection." Am Psychol 50 (3).

Buss, D. M., and D. P. Schmitt (1993). "Sexual strategies theory: An evolutionary perspective on human mating." Psychol Rev 100 (2).

Chomsky Noam, (2016) Who Rules the World?

Chomsky Noam, and Pappe Ilan, (2010) Gaza in Crisis: Reflections On Israel's War against the Palestinians. Haymarket Books.

Churchland, P.S. (1986), Neurophilosophy (Cambridge, MA: The MIT Press).

Churchland, P.S. & Ramachandran, V.S. (1993), 'Filling in: Why Dennett is wrong', in Dennett and His Critics: Demystifying Mind, ed. B. Dahlbom (Oxford: Blackwell Scientific Press).

Churchland, P.S., Ramachandran, V.S. & Sejnowski, T.J. (1994), 'A critique of pure vision', in Large- scale Neuronal Theories of the Brain, ed. C. Koch & J.L. Davis (Cambridge, MA: The MIT Press).

Crick, F. (1994), The Astonishing Hypothesis: The Scientific Search for the Soul (New York: Simon and Schuster).

Crick, F. (1996), 'Visual perception: rivalry and consciousness', Nature, 379.

Crick, F. & Koch, C. (1992), 'The problem of consciousness', Scientific American, 267.

d'Aquili, Eugene. "Senses of Reality in Science and Religion." Zygon 17, no 4 (1982)

d'Aquili, Eugene. "The Biopsychological Determinants of Religious Ritual Behavior." Zygon 10, no. 1 (1975)

d'Aquili, Eugene. "The Myth-Ritual Complex: A Biogenetic Structural Analysis." Zygon 18, no. 3 (1983)

d'Aquili, Eugene, and Andrew Newberg. The Mystical Mind: Probing the Biology of Religious Experience. Minneapolis: Fortress Press, 1999.

Damasio, A. (1994) Descartes' Error: Emotion, Reason and the Human Brain. New York, Putnams.

Damasio, A. (1999) The Feeling of What Happens: Body, Emotion and the Making of Consciousness. London, Heinemann.

Darwin, C. (1859) On the Origin of Species by Means of Natural Selection. London, Murray.

Darwin, C. (1871) The Descent of Man and Selection in Relation to Sex. London, John Murray.

Dawkins, R. (1976) The Selfish Gene. Oxford, Oxford University Press; a new edition, with additional material, was published in 1989.

Dewhurst, Kenneth, and A. W. Beard. "Sudden Religious Conversions in Temporal Lobe Epilepsy." British Journal of Psychiatry 117 (1970)

Dewhurst K, Beard AW. Sudden religious conversions in temporal lobe epilepsy. 1970 Epilepsy Behav 2003

Devinsky O, Lai G. Spirituality and religion in epilepsy. Epilepsy Behav 2008.

E. Horvitz, "One Hundred Year Study on Artificial Intelligence: Reflections and Framing," ed: Stanford University, 2014.

Eckhart Meister, Selected Writings

Farah, M.J. (1989), 'The neural basis of mental imagery', Trends in Neurosciences, 10.

Freud, S. "Selected papers on hysteria and other psychoneuroses" Journal of Nervous and Mental Disease 1909.

Freud, S. "The Origin and Development of Psychoanalysis", 1910

Freud, S. "Psychopathology of everyday life", 1914

Freud, S. "Beyond the Pleasure Principle", 1920

Frith, C.D. & Dolan, R.J. (1997), 'Abnormal beliefs: Delusions and memory', Paper presented at the May, 1997, Harvard Conference on Memory and Belief.

Gay, Volney, ed. Neuroscience and Religion. Plymouth, UK: Lexington Books, 2009.

Gazzaniga, M. S. (1985). The social brain. New York: Basic Books.

Gazzaniga, M.S. (1993), 'Brain mechanisms and conscious experience', Ciba Foundation Symposium, 174.

Geschwind N. "Behavioural changes in temporal lobe epilepsy". Psychol Med. 1979.

Gellhorn, E., Kiely, W.F. "Mystical states of consciousness: neurophysiological and clinical aspects." J Nerv Ment Dis. 1972;154:399-405.

Gilbert SL, Dobyns WB, Lahn BT (2005) Genetic links between brain development and brain evolution. Nat Rev Genet 6.

Gray JA. The Psychology of Fear and Stress. 2nd ed. New York, NY: Cambridge University Press; 1988.

Gloor, P. (1992), 'Amygdala and temporal lobe epilepsy', in The Amygdala: Neurobiological Aspects of Emotion, Memory and Mental Dysfunction, ed J.P. Aggleton (New York: Wiley-Liss).

Gross CG, Rocha-Miranda CE, Bender DB (1972) Visual properties of neurons in the inferotemporal cortex of the macaque. J Neurophysiol 35: 96–111.

Guevara Che, The Motorcycle Diaries, 1992

Hardy, G. H. (1940). Ramanujan. Cambridge: Cambridge University Press.

Hall, Daniel, Keith Meador, and Harold Koenig. "Measuring Religiousness in Health Research: Review and Critique." Journal of Religion and Health 47, no. 2 (2008)

Harris, Sam, Jonas Kaplan, Ashley Curiel, Susan Bookheimer, Marco Iacoboni, and Mark Cohen. "The Neural Correlates of Religious and Nonreligious Belief." PLoS One 4, no. 10 (October 1, 2009)

Halgren, E. (1992), 'Emotional neurophysiology of the amygdala within the context of human cognition', in The Amygdala: Neurobiological Aspects of Emotion, Memory and Mental Dysfunction, ed J.P. Aggleton (New York: Wiley-Liss).

Halligan PW, Fink GR, Marshal JC, Vallar G. 2003. Spatial cognition: evidence from visual neglect. Trends Cogn Sci.

Handbook of Emotions, Edited by Michael Lewis, Jeannette M. Haviland-Jones, and Lisa Feldman Barrett, The Guilford Press; 3rd edition (2010).

Hameroff, S.R. and Penrose, R. (1996) Conscious events as orchestrated space-time selections. Journal of Consciousness Studies 3(1), 36-53; also reprinted in J. Shear (ed.) (1997) Explaining Consciousness-The Hard Problem. Cambridge, MA, MIT Press, 177-95.

Harding, D.E. (1961) On Having no Head: Zen and the Re-Discovery of the Obvious. London, Buddhist Society.

Hardy, A. (1979) The Spiritual Nature of Man: A Study of Contemporary Religious Experience. Oxford, Clarendon Press.

Harre, R. and Gillett, G. (1994) The Discursive Mind. Thousand Oaks, CA, Sage.

Haugeland, J. (ed.) (1997) Mind Design II: Philosophy, Psychology, Artificial Intelligence. Cambridge, MA, MIT Press.

Hauser, M.D. (2000) Wild Minds: What Animals Really Think. New York, Henry Holt and Co.; London, Penguin.

Hilgard, E.R. (1986) Divided Consciousness: Multiple Controls in Human Thought and Action. New York, Wiley.

Hilton, E.N., Lundberg, T.R. Transgender Women in the Female Category of Sport: Perspectives on Testosterone Suppression and Performance Advantage. Sports Med 51, 199–214 (2021).

Hitler, Adolf. Mein Kampf, 1925

Hodgson, R. (1891) A case of double consciousness. Proceedings of the Society for Psychical Research 7, 221-58.

Hofstadter, D.R. and Dennett, D.C. (eds) (1981) The Mind's I: Fantasies and Reflections on Self and Soul. London, Penguin.

Holland, J. (ed.) (2001) Ecstasy: The Complete Guide: A Comprehensive Look at the Risks and Benefits of

MDMA. Rochester, VT, Park Street Press.

Holmes, D.S. (1987) The influence of meditation versus rest on physiological arousal. In M. West (ed.) The Psychology of Meditation. Oxford, Clarendon Press, 81-103.

Holmstrom, David. 1992, Christian Science Monitor

Holloway RL (1996) Evolution of the human brain. In: Lock A, Peters CR (eds) Handbook of human symbolic evolution. Oxford University Press, Oxford

Jablonski, Nina G. 2006. Skin: A Natural History. Berkeley, CA: University of California Press.

Jeannerod M (1988) The neural and behavioural organization of goal-directed movements. Clarendon Press, Oxford.

Johnson-Frey SH, Maloof FR, Newman-Norlund R, Farrer C, Inati S, Grafton ST (2003) Actions or hand-objects interactions? Human inferior frontal cortex and action observation. Neuron 39: 1053–1058.

Jackson, F. (1982) Epiphenomenal qualia. Philosophical Quarterly 32, 127-36.

James, W. (1890) The Principles of Psychology (2 volumes). London, Macmillan.

James, W. (1902) The Varieties of Religious Experience: A Study in Human Nature. New York and London, Longmans, Green and Co.

Jansen, K. (2001) Ketamine: Dreams and Realities. Sarasota, FL, Multidisciplinary Association for Psychedelic Studies.

Jay, M. (ed.) (1999) Artificial Paradises: A Drugs Reader. London, Penguin.

Jaynes, J. (1976) The Origin of Consciousness in the Breakdown of the Bicameral Mind. New York, Houghton Mifflin.

Kandel, E. R. In Search of Memory: The Emergence of a New Science of Mind, W. W. Norton & Company (2007).

Kandel E. R. Schwartz JH, Jessel TM. Principles of neural sciences. New York; McGraw Hill, 2000.

Kanwisher, N. (2001) Neural events and perceptual awareness. Cognition 79, 89-113; also reprinted inS. Dehaene (ed.) The Cognitive Neuroscience of Consciousness. Cambridge, MA, MIT Press, 89-113.

Kihlstrom, J.F. (1996) Perception without awareness of what is perceived, learning without awareness of what is learned. In M. Velmans (ed.) The Science of Consciousness. London, Routledge, 23-46.

Kosslyn, S.M. (1980) Image and Mind. Cambridge, MA, Harvard University Press.

Kosslyn, S.M. (1988) Aspects of a cognitive neuroscience of mental imagery. Science 240, 1621-6.

Kjaer, Troels, Camilla Bertelsen, Paola Piccini, David Brooks, Jorgen Alving, and Hans Lou. "Increased Dopamine Tone during Meditation- Induced Change of Consciousness." Cognitive Brain Research 13, no. 2 (April 2002)

Kölmel HW. 1985. Complex visual hallucinations in the hemianopic field. J Neurol Neurosurg Psychiatry.

Koenig, Harold. "Research on Religion, Spirituality, and Mental Health: A Review." Canadian Journal of Psychiatry 54, no. 5 (May 2009)

Koenig, Harold, ed. Handbook of Religion and Mental Health. San Diego, CA: Academic Press, 1998

Kraepelin E. Psychiatry: A Textbook for Students and Physicians. New York, NY: Science History Publications; 1990.

Lauglin, Charles, John McManus, and Eugene d'Aquili. Brain, Symbol, and Experience. 2nd ed. New York: Columbia University Press, 1992

Lakoff, G. and M. Johnson (1999). Philosophy in the flesh. Basic Books: New York.

LeDoux, J. E. (1996). The emotional brain. New York: Simon & Schuster.

LeDoux, J.E. (1992), 'Emotion and the amygdala', in The Amygdala: Neurobiological Aspects of Emo- tion, Memory and Mental Dysfunction, ed J.P. Aggleton (New York: Wiley-Liss).

Levin, D.T. and Simons, D.J. (1997) Failure to detect changes to attended objects in motion pictures. Psychonomic Bulletin and Review 4, 501-6.

Levine,J. (1983) Materialism and qualia: the explanatory gap. Pacific Philosophical Quarterly 64, 354-61.

Levine,J. (2001) Purple Haze: The Puzzle of Consciousness. New York, Oxford University Press. Levine, S. (1979) A Gradual Awakening. New York, Doubleday.

Levinson, B.W. (1965) States of awareness during general anaesthesia. British Journal of Anaesthesia 37, 544-6.

Lewicki, P., Czyzewska, M. and Hoffman, H. (1987) Unconscious acquisition of complex procedural knowledge. Journal of Experimental Psychology: Learning, Memory and Cognition 13, 523-30.

Naskar, Abhijit. "What is Mind?", 2016

Naskar, Abhijit. "Love, God & Neurons: Memoir of A Scientist who found himself by getting lost", 2016

Naskar, Abhijit. "Principia Humanitas", 2017

Naskar, Abhijit. "We Are All Black: A Treatise on Racism", 2017

Naskar, Abhijit. "Either Civilized or Phobic: A Treatise on Homosexuality", 2017

Naskar, Abhijit. "Build Bridges not Walls: In the name of Americana", 2018

Naskar, Abhijit. "Citizens of Peace: Beyond the Savagery of Sovereignty", 2019

Naskar, Abhijit. "The Constitution of The United Peoples of Earth", 2019

Naskar, Abhijit. "Mission Reality", 2019

Naskar, Abhijit. "Good Scientist: When Science and Service Combine", 2020

Newberg, Andrew, and Jeremy Iversen. "The Neural Basis of the

Complex Mental Task of Meditation: Neurotransmitter and Neurochemical Considerations." Medical Hypotheses 61, no. 2 (2003).

Newberg, Andrew. "How God Changes Your Brain: An Introduction to Jewish Neurotheology", CCAR Journal: The Reform Jewish Quarterly, Winter 2016.

Newberg, Andrew, and Stephanie Newberg. "A Neuropsychological Perspective on Spiritual Development." In Handbook of Spiritual Development in Childhood and Adolescence, edited by Eugene Roehlkepartain, Pamela King, Linda Wagener, and Peter Benson. London: Sage Publications, Inc., 2005

Newberg, Andrew. "The Neurotheology Link An Intersection Between Spirituality and Health", Alternative and Complimentary Therapies, Vol 21 No 1, February 2015.

Newberg, Andrew, Nancy Wintering, Dharma Khalsa, Hannah Roggenkamp, and Mark Waldman. "Meditation Effects on Cognitive Function and Cerebral Blood Flow in Subjects with Memory Loss: A Preliminary Study." Journal of Alzheimer's Disease 20, no. 2 (2010)

Nash, M. (1995), 'Glimpses of the mind', Time.

Nesse RM. Proximate and evolutionary studies of anxiety, stress and depression: synergy at the interface. Neurosci Biobehav Rev. 1999;23:895-903.

Nicolelis, Miguel. (2011) "Beyond Boundaries: The New Neuroscience of Connecting Brains with Machines--- and How It Will Change Our Lives", Times Books

O'Hara, K. and Scutt, T. (1996) There is no hard problem of consciousness. Journal of Consciousness Studies 3(4),

290-302, reprinted in J. Shear (ed.) (1997) Explaining Consciousness. Cambridge, MA, MIT Press, 69-82.

O'Regan, J.K. and Noe, A. (2001) A sensorimotor account of vision and visual consciousness. Behavioral and Brain Sciences 24(5), 883-917.

Ornstein, R.E. (1977) The Psychology of Consciousness (2nd edn). New York, Harcourt.

Ornstein, R.E. (1986) The Psychology of Consciousness (3rd edn). New York, Pehguin.

Ornstein, R.E. (1992) The Evolution of Consciousness. New York, Touchstone.

Penfield W, Faulk ME (1955) The insula: further observations on its function. Brain 78: 445– 470.

Penrose, R. (1994), Shadows of the Mind (Oxford: Oxford University Press).

Penrose, R. (1989), The Emperor's New Mind: Concerning Computers, Minds and The Laws of Physics (Oxford: Oxford University Press).

Persinger, "'I would kill in God's name' role of sex, weekly church attendance, report of a religious experience and limbic lability" Perceptual and Motor Skills 1997.

Persinger "Experimental simulation of the God experience" Neurotheology 2003.

Persinger, Corradini, Clement, Keaney, et al "Neurotheology and its convergence with neuroquantology" NeuroQuantology 2010.

Persinger. "The neuropsychiatry of paranormal experiences". J Neuropsychiatry Clin Neurosci 2001.

Persinger. "Neuropsychological bases of god beliefs", New York: Praeger, 1987

Persinger. "Temporal lobe epileptic signs and correlative behaviors displayed by normal populations", Journal of General Psychology, 1986

Perry BD, Pollard R. Homeostasis, stress, trauma, and adaptation. A neurodevelopmental view of childhood trauma. Child Adolesc Psychiatr Clin N Am. 1998;7:33.

Ramachandran VS. Behavioral and magnetoencephalographic correlates of plasticity in the adult human brain. Proc Natl Acad Sci USA 1993; 90: 10413–20.

Ramachandran VS. Plasticity and functional recovery in neurology. Clin Med 2005; 5: 368–73.

Rock I, Victor J. Vision and touch: an experimentally created conflict between the two senses. Science 1964; 143: 594–6.

Roberts, TA; Smalley, J; Ahrendt, D (December 2020). "Effect of gender affirming hormones on athletic performance in transwomen and transmen: implications for sporting organisations and legislators". British Journal of Sports Medicine. 55 (11): 577–583

Royet JP, Plailly J, Delon-Martin C, Kareken DA, Segebarth C (2003) fMRI of emotional responses to odors: influence of hedonic valence and judgment, handedness, and gender. Neuroimage 20: 713–728.

Rozin R Haidt J and McCauley CR (2000) Disgust. In: Lewis M, Haviland-Jones JM (eds) Handbook of Emotion. 2nd Edition. Guilford Press, New York, pp 637–653.

Saxe R, Carey S, Kanwisher N (2004) Understanding other minds: linking developmental psychology and functional neuroimaging. Annu Rev Psychol 55: 87–124.

S. J. Russell and P. Norvig, Artificial intelligence: a modern approach (3rd edition): Prentice Hall, 2009.

Singer T, Seymour B, O'Doherty J, Kaube H, Dolan RJ, Frith CD (2004) Empathy for pain involves the affective but not the sensory components of pain. Science 303: 1157–1162.

Smith A (1759) The theory of moral sentiments (ed. 1976). Clarendon Press, Oxford.

Schilling, Vincent. 2017, indian country today

Stein, Stephen K. 2017, The Sea in World History: Exploration, Travel, and Trade

Tesla N. "My Inventions", 1919

T. R. Society, "Machine learning: the power and promise of computers that learn by example," ed. The Royal Society, 2017.

Tomasello M, Call J (1997) Primate cognition. Oxford University Press, Oxford

185

187

189